I0841107

ACKNOWLEDGMENTS

I would like to thank Debbie Garcia, Toni Smith, Lauriana Soden, and Murray Davis in providing their perspective.

And, a special thanks to my wife.

Ray

We come together in relationships to grow and not live in misery. Here are some of the reasons it's difficult to find someone worthy of a committed relationship:

- We haven't truly ended the last one and must learn to close the door on old relationships
- We hold on to romantic memories and special times with others, not letting go
- With all the things we hold on to, how can we expect others to get into our hearts
- Sort through your own garbage, clearing your heart and mind to receive a new partner
- Never make anyone responsible for your happiness
- Be realistic about your expectations
- Trust how your inner self feels, that gut feeling
- Play close attention to the warning signs and/or red flags

Remember, the 5 things that most women want from men are **RESPECT, HONESTY, TRUST RELIABILITY, AND PLAYFULNESS.**

PREFACE

Gentlemen, the RULE of thumb is...

If a woman meets 10 men, 80% of them are considered losers, jerks, or playboys. Be the exception and not the 80%.

A healthy relationship is a 100 / 100 proposition. Each partner gives 100%

The only way out of any problem is the truth!

CONTENTS

MEETING SOMEONE

CHAPTER 1

1. Always act as if your mother or someone you highly respect is standing next to you

2. Look the person in the eye but don't stare

3. Offer a firm handshake and no fist bumping

4. Don't introduce yourself by your nickname, i.e., KC or DJ

5. Say good morning, afternoon, or evening

6. Don't judge, you will never know until you find out

7. Know how to dress, attire is always important

8. Articulate clearly and speak with conviction

9. Learn a little handy work like painting, plumbing, assembly, hammering, or simply emptying the trash

10. Know how to check a car's oil or change a tire

11. Be willing to give everyone a fresh start

MEETING A WOMAN

CHAPTER 2

1. Introduce yourself and wait for her to extend her hand, keeping in mind some women don't care to shake hands

2. Don't use profanity, it makes a bad impression

3. Don't stare at her, it makes her feel uncomfortable

4. Be yourself and if you are shy, outgoing, or boring, she will know sooner or later

5. Allow people to show themselves, you would rather know now rather than later

6. Accept people for who they are, if they are not for you, move on

7. Always find something nice to say about a woman even if you're not interested

8. Never refer to women as bitches or hoes, even
    when you are male bonding, you never know who
    is listening

9. If you happen to get her phone number, don't call
    before 9:00 am or after 9:00 pm unless she asks
    you too

CHAPTER 3
OUT ON A DATE

1. Never ask a woman to your place as a first date

2. If you ask her out, you should pay, however if she
    asks you out you may want to discuss expenses
    to be very clear

3. On the first date ask her to meet you, it makes her
    feel safe, otherwise let her decide

4. Always be fresh out of the shower and if you wear
    cologne go light rather than heavy

5. Be on time, it doesn't look good when your date
    is waiting, and if you're running late contact her

6.   Know how to dress on your date, asking her if necessary, or use common sense

7.   Don't wear a baseball hat unless you are going to the ball game

8.   Do not judge her even if you meet her on a blind date, we all have ways to express ourselves

9.   If you pick her up at her place, meet her at the door, don't call her from the car, honk your horn, or text her, unless she asks you to

10. Be considerate, drive safe, and keep your car clean

11. Don't play loud music

12. Chivalry isn't dead so use your best judgment when you need to open her door

13. Don't talk too much, let her get some words in, but also don't bore her

14. Don't go overboard trying to impress her by bragging

15. Listen to her and don't interrupt

16. Walk on the street side so that you can protect her

17. Don't hold hands, it's too early

18. Don't be a know-it-all, if you don't know
     something just say you don't know

19. Let her order first and don't criticize what she
     orders

20. When together, stay off the phone, yes that also
     means texting, it's disrespectful

21. Respectfully compliment her but don't go
     overboard

22. If she meets you at the date, walk her to the car

23   If she finds it convenient to drive to your place for
     the date, you must drive your car to the date
     unless she wants to drive her car, and do not
     invite her into your place

24. If she valet parked at the date, wait with her until
     the valet brings her car and tip the valet

25. At the end of the date don't pressure her, let it
     flow

26. Don't expect to kiss her, a nice hug or handshake
     will do

27. Be patient with overeager women

CHAPTER 4

AT YOUR PLACE

1. Keep your place clean, first impressions matter

2. Ask her if she needs anything, making her comfortable

3. Don't take her on a tour unless she asks

4. If the phone rings, let it go to voicemail, or excuse yourself to answer just for a few minutes

5. Use phone etiquette even if you know who is calling. Don't say "what" or "what's up"

6. If you play music, play something soft and upbeat

7. If you turn on the television don't just watch what you want, you have a guest now

8. Ask and talk about her choice of music

9. Keep the day or evening flowing

10. Do not pressure her

11.   Feel comfortable respectfully ending the date

12.   When leaving, walk her to the car and ask her to call or text you when she gets home

13.   If she stays overnight, let her choose where to sleep

CHAPTER 5 - AT HER PLACE

1.   Never arrive at a woman's house for the first time empty handed, present her with a bottle of wine, a box of chocolates, etc. to show you have some class

2.   Don't just flop on the couch and put your feet up because this is a turn off

3.   Don't help yourself to the refrigerator, that's rude

4.   When using her bathroom always lift the toilet seat and lower it when done, if necessary

5.   If you have to do "big things" in her bathroom, do a courtesy flush as soon as you drop and use a spray air freshener or light a match, it helps with the smell

6.   Let her call the shots, you are the guest

7.   Be respectful if she's too assertive, remember you want a worthy committed relationship

CHAPTER 6
IN HER CAR

1. Don't be a driver in the passenger seat, if she wants your help she will ask

2. Don't shout at people through the window

3. Don't ask her to make a stop, unless otherwise

4. Don't change the radio station without asking

5. If she stops for gas, ask her if she needs anything, always pump the gas, pay if you want, and clean the windows

6. Talk to her while she is driving, it helps her to stay alert and keeps you both from getting bored

7. Don't read a book or play with your electronic devices while she is driving unless you include her

CHAPTER 7 - DATING

1. Keep the dates interesting, role playing is sometimes an option

2. After a dinner or movie take a short walk just to talk plus it helps to walk off a big meal

3. Ask if she would like to hold hands

4. Don't always take the same route, it's boring

5. Be spontaneous

6. Call or text her the next day to say you enjoyed her company

7. Pay attention to her and get an idea about the little things she likes and dislikes

8. Don't change yourself to mirror her likes or dislikes, the true you will eventually come out

9. When a woman says "no", it only means one thing

10. Make her feel like she's your women, respect her

11. It doesn't' matter how powerful a woman is, she loves to feel safe when it comes to her man

12. If she doesn't answer one of your many texts, it means you may be texting too much

13. Don't bother her at work, if she has the time she will call you or you can text her

14. If she is really upset with you, take her to a public place or restaurant to talk

15. If your home or car smells like you, you either wear too much cologne or not bathing enough

16. Don't crowd her, give her space

17. Admit your mistakes, stop trying to defend yourself, and learn to apologize

18. Never use the word "but" in an apology, it destroys the whole purpose

19. Keep the romance alive and stay youthful

20. When she shows you how she is, trust her, remember you want a worthy committed relationship

21. Before you fall asleep kiss her goodnight and when you wake up give her a light touch and say good morning

22. Understand that conflict is normal in a relationship, but you can't fix it unless you face it

23. Women like to talk through problems, men would rather move on so talk to her and listen

24. Get close after every
     disagreement

25. Dating is a grace period
     before a commitment

26. Make sure she's into you, if she's not it will not
     work out, you're wasting your time

27. Make it clear that you're dating to just date, dating
     to get married, etc. so there are no
     misunderstandings

28. If you are not into her, let her know and don't
     waste her time or lead her on

29. If she doesn't appreciate you just move on and
     wish her the best

30. If breaking it off don't say "it's not you", you can
     say something like "I'm not the man for you"

31. Don't be disrespectful or say bad things simply
     because it didn't work out

32. Before you consider marriage think about all the
     compromises you will have to make and if it's
     worth it, if not you're not ready

33. If you tell her that you love her it means you
     want the best for her whether or not you're
     included

34. When going to bed, hold hands

CHAPTER 8 - LIVING TOGETHER

1. Set aside time to discuss and plan expenses

2. Share things, don't say this is mine or this is yours

3. Respect each other's time, space, property and friendships

4. Share responsibilities and don't let her do it all

5. Don't wait for her to ask you for help, remember it's a partnership

6. If you are going to be late coming home let her know as soon as possible to build trust

7. Let her have a night or day to do whatever she wants, women love to pamper themselves and at times need alone time too

8. Some women need maintenance and attention so don't grumble about it, embrace it

9. Stay in shape and try to maintain healthy eating habits because it motivates her

CHAPTER 9
MARRIAGE

It's easy to get married but it's not easy to stay married so be good to one another. When you say "I DO, MAKE SURE YOU DO" #VOWS

Everything mentioned in the previous chapters also apply when married. Here are some common sense key pointers for a successful union to consider:

1. Spirituality/Faith/Religion

2. Respect

3. Transparent Communication

4. Compromise

5. Affection

6. Laughter/Fun

7. Healthy sex life

8. Financially responsible

9. Overall compatibility

CHAPTER 10
KIDS

1. If you decide to have kids, make sure you are in complete agreement and you are prepared to commit to parenthood with or without each other because it may not work out

2. If she has kids, be prepared to love them as well, be willing, accepting, and respectful as your ability to compromise and your patience will be tested

3. If you are not sure about the above, you may not be ready

4. Additional information on this topic is an entirely different book

CHAPTER 11 - LAST TIDBITS

1. Be a man of principle and learn as much as you can

2. Learn to become a good kisser with fresh breath

3. Avoid foolish and ignorant disputes

4. Relationships take deep communication to change and even deeper commitment to grow

5. Try not to raise your voice when you're upset

6. Get in the habit of saying please and thank you

7. Don't be lazy, it sets a bad example

8. Don't be a complainer or act like a victim, change what you can and accept what you can't

9. Never ask a woman her age, weight, salary unless she brings it up

10. It takes a lot of courage to admit when a relationship is not working, accept it, let go, and move on without being rude

11. Making a difficult decision can make us feel miserable, but not making it can lead to more pain

12. If you don't let go, good things will never happen

13. Try to meet each other's needs, ask her what she needs from you and tell her what you need from her, within reason

14. Accept that you may have a problem, because the way we live is a reflection of our accepted bad behavior

15. If you want to be in a relationship and you've never been married, or have no kids, take a look at yourself

16. There is someone out there for everyone so try not to settle

17. Don't chase a woman, if she wants you she will make it known

18. Love is patient, Love is kind, and it is most certainly not mentally or physically abusive

19. Don't try to change a person, they will change if they want to

20. If you don't respect yourself, how is anyone else supposed to respect you

BEST OF LUCK!